How To Get Married And Survive It

A Guide to Wedding, Reception, and Honeymoon Planning

Beth L. Hilton

Illustrated by Val C. Bagley

INTERNATIONAL STANDARD BOOK NUMBER
0-88290-148-6

Printed and Distributed in the
United States of America
by

**Horizon
Publishers &
Distributors**

P.O. Box 490
50 South 500 West
Bountiful, Utah 84010

CONTENTS

3

HOW TO GET MARRIED AND SURVIVE IT

How To Get Married And Survive It

Love—isn't it wonderful! The birds sing, bells ring, rainbows appear in the sky. The lovers acquire a special glow, and seem to live in a world of enchantment all their own. When they reach that stage, marriage is not far away. But weddings, today, are complex events, and they require careful preparation if they are to be the joyful occasions we all want them to be.

The months preceding a young couple's wedding can be hectic and hurried, or they can be fun-filled and enjoyable for the bride and groom-to-be. The key to making these months pleasant and productive is proper planning. If everyone has some way of knowing what needs to be done and when to do it, a lovely and memorable wedding is on it's way.

A wedding can and should be one of life's most cherished experiences. Poor planning and lack of knowledge should not be allowed to mar this momentous occasion.

It is for this purpose that this booklet was written. By following its guidelines and utilizing its planning checklist, the bride and groom-to-be should be well on their way to realizing the wedding and reception of their dreams.

Contact Between the Families of the Bride and Groom

There simply can't be enough communication between families of the bride and the groom. Good communication

---

■ *Love doesn't make the world go around. Love is what makes the ride worthwhile.*

will help to avoid many possible problems in the planning of a wedding and reception. When the families live in different areas, this becomes more difficult, but still is very important. If the families have not become acquainted before the engagement, the parents of the groom should contact the parents of the bride very shortly after wedding plans are announced. If the distance permits, this should be a personal visit, usually with the bridal couple present. The bride's parents should return the call within a comfortable length of time. Many basic plans and decisions can be made during these meetings. Before the couple selects their invitations, for instance, both sets of parents should have imput concerning how they would like their names printed on them. The bride and her mother should take special care to inform the groom's family, especially his mother, of the plans for the wedding and reception. If an open house is planned by the groom's family, she will want to co-ordinate her plans with yours. The considerate bride will also make the groom's parents aware of gifts sent by friends and relatives of the groom's family.

Initial Interview with Bishop

Whether they are planning a temple or a civil marriage, an LDS couple should schedule an interview with their Bishop at the earliest possible opportunity to discuss plans for the wedding. He can help prepare them for the coming wedding and answer any questions they might have. This initial interview is not for the purpose of obtaining a temple recommend. It is important at this time, however, to have your Bishop concur with your temple wedding plans so that this information can be put on your invitations.

Making the Guest List

The guest list is the responsibility of the bride's mother, with the help of the bride; and the groom's mother, with the help of the groom. The groom and his mother should send their lists, complete with addresses, to the bride's mother as soon after the engagement is announced as possible. Working with

---

■*Love may be blind, but your mother-in-law isn't.*

the list will be easier if the bride has been able to go over it with the groom's mother. An approach many couples use is for the bride to set up an alphabetical card file, with a separate card for each invitation to be sent. This file can be expanded to include information on gifts received and thank-you notes sent, becoming a permanent address record for the new family or being returned to the parents as a beginning list for their next family wedding.

Reserving Reception Facilities

It is important to make arrangements for the use of the reception center, meetinghouse, friend or relative's home, etc. as soon after deciding on a wedding day as possible in order to insure its availability for the reception. Because most reception facilities can host no more than one reception a night, and popular dates are reserved many months in advance, it might be necessary when reserving the facility to first ask what nights are available and then select the date. Friends and relatives should not be informed of the date or location of the reception until after this has been done. It is advisable to put a deposit down to reserve the reception facility. Remember to plan for an alternate site in case of rain if a garden reception is being scheduled.

Scheduling the Wedding Ceremony

If they plan to be married in the temple, the couple must call or write to the temple of their choice. The temple staff will

■*It should be every man's goal to afford what he is spending.*

send the information necessary for setting the date and the hour of the wedding. If you plan to have anyone other than assigned personnel perform your ceremony, you must also schedule your wedding with them. The Temple personnel will allow the definite time of day for the wedding to be scheduled about a month before it is to take place. The marriage ceremony will take about one-half hour. If you plan to have a civil wedding, it is necessary to contact your Bishop or other church official to schedule and make arrangements for the ceremony. The wedding is usually performed by the bride's bishop or clergyman, rather than the groom's, since the wedding is the responsibility of her family.

Inviting Attendants to Participate in the Wedding Party

The honor of being an attendant in a wedding party is bestowed on close relatives and friends of the bride and groom. Since it is impossible to schedule the reception at the best time for all of your attendants, the date and time of the reception should be set by the bridal couple before their attendants are asked to participate. Then they can know if their personal schedules will allow them to accept. The bride may choose either a maid of honor (usually an unmarried sister or close friend of about the same age) or a matron of honor (usually a married sister or close friend of about the same age). She also may select bridesmaids. These are usually her own sisters, sisters of the groom, and close friends and relatives. If she desires, the bride may also have a flower girl, who is a young sister, relative, or friend.

The groom selects a best man. The best man can be the groom's father, brother, or close friend. The groom also chooses ushers, with one sometimes being designated as head usher. These are usually his own brothers, brothers of the bride, or close friends and relatives who greet guests and direct them as to where they should go.

Announcing the Engagement in the Newspaper

This is optional. If it is desired, the announcement should be made by the parents of the bride or by a close relative,

■*Nowadays, two can live as cheaply as one large family used to.*

guardian, or friend if the bride's parents are deceased. The article should be typed double spaced on a sheet of white paper with the release date clearly written at the top of the page. A picture of the engaged girl may be sent with the announcement. Many newspapers charge for printing a picture with the announcement. Some newspapers also have the policy to print either the engagement announcement or the wedding story, but *not* both. Your local newspaper should be contacted to find out its rules.

Scheduling the Rehearsal

A rehearsal of the wedding ceremony is not necessary for a temple marriage and is not held. The temple ceremony is simple and there are competent temple personnel there to assist the couple and the members of the wedding party.

However, if a civil ceremony is planned, it is wise to contact the official performing the ceremony to schedule a rehearsal for the wedding party. The rehearsal often takes place on the evening before the wedding ceremony and is conducted by the person who will perform the wedding. Rehearsals usually are not held in civil marriages performed by LDS Bishops, though the Bishop will usually outline the procedure in detail to the couple who is to be wed.

Making Arrangements for the Wedding Breakfast or Rehearsal Dinner

The parents of the groom usually host the wedding breakfast or luncheon, or the rehearsal dinner (if a rehearsal is called for). The wedding breakfast or luncheon, or dinner follows the marriage ceremony and may either be held at a restaurant or in a home or meetinghouse. Reservations at a popular restaurant need to be made well in advance. If the wedding is to be held in a temple, it is important to check the schedule carefully so the meal can be scheduled at the correct hour.

Operators of reception centers sometimes point out the advantages of holding the wedding breakfast, luncheon or dinner, as well as the reception, in their facility. The wedding party will usually be the only customers present, so they will have

■*A diamond is a chunk of coal that made good under pressure.*
(Classic Crossword Puzzles)

ample parking, no time nor space limitations, and they will receive the full attention and service of the facility personnel. In contrast, a restaurant may be crowded and the service personnel may have to divide their attention several directions.

If the meal is to be provided by friends or relatives, it will be best if it is prepared by people not attending the ceremony. The guests expected at this dinner should include the wedding party and special friends personally invited by the bridal couple.

The wedding rehearsal dinner is usually held the evening before the ceremony at a local restaurant, meetinghouse, or home. If a rehearsal is held the morning of the wedding day, the dinner follows at about noon, the wedding at about 5:00, and the reception at about 7:00. This schedule may vary considerably.

Ordering or Beginning Construction of Wedding Gown and Attendants' Gowns

This is the time for the bride to be her most beautiful self. She is the focal point of the day, and the right wedding gown will lend magic to the event.  The attendants' gowns will add to the beautiful picture to be created, and should harmonize with the dress plan for the entire wedding party. There are several approaches to obtaining the wedding gown and the gowns of the attendants. These dresses may be bought, sewn by a professional, or sewn by the bride and her attendants or their mothers. In some areas, these dresses may even be rented. If the bride plans to wear her wedding dress in the temple, it must have a high neck (or dickey), a long skirt, and wrist-length sleeves. The temple has lovely wedding dresses that may be rented for the ceremony only. The attendants' gowns usually should all be alike and should compliment the style of the bride's gown.

■*It is a funny thing about life. If you refuse to accept anything but the best, you very often get it.* (Somerset Maugham)

The wedding gown should be completed at least six weeks prior to the wedding so the bridal portrait can be taken.

Decisions concerning the style and color of the clothing to be worn by the groom and his assistants should be made as the color scheme for the reception line is being determined.

Arranging for Receptions and Openhouses Out of Town

If the bride and groom are from different cities, the decision may be made to hold both a reception and an openhouse. Typically, the bride and her family pay for the reception (except for the boutonnieres and bouquets, which usually are still handled by the groom) and the groom and his family pay for the openhouse. If this is the case, the groom's family is responsible for making all the arrangements for the openhouse, just as the bride's family is responsible for the reception. Usually the same colors and clothing are planned for both places. The companies which rent tuxedos will usually allow the rental period to be extended to cover both events.

Engaging and Meeting with the Photographer

Wedding days pass rather quickly, but quality pictures can help capture the happy memories. Photographs of the reception and other wedding day events may either be taken by a friend with a talent for photography or by a professional photographer. Professional work should not be expected from a friend, so it is desirable to hire a professional, if possible. Professional photographers usually make package offers from which the couple may choose. These packages are often less expensive if the choice is made to have the same photographer take the engagement and newspaper photographs and the formal wedding portraits as well. Whether a friend or a professional is chosen, it is important to meet with the photographer and discuss prices, scheduling, and the pictures desired well in advance of the wedding day. If other people are to be allowed or invited to take pictures at the same time a professional photographer is working (either at the temple or just

By all means, marry. If you get a good wife, you'll become happy. If you get a bad one, you'll become a philosopher.
(Socrates)

before the reception begins), the photographer should be aware of these plans. He might not want to work with others around and it could prevent bad feelings for all concerned if the matter is discussed and other arrangements are made if necessary.

Engaging and Meeting with the Caterer

A caterer can save the bride and her parents many hours of work, worry, and frustration. He is able to offer as much or as little help as they desire. A good, well-established caterer can take care of the wedding invitations, napkins, thank-you cards, the guestbook, the wedding cake, food (including all tables, centerpieces, serving trays, cups, and spoons), decorations, flowers, the wedding dress, tuxedos, and perhaps even the photography. Most caterers are prepared to offer a package deal that results in real savings if all of their services are utilized rather than contracting each item separately. It is wise to meet with one or several caterers to see what they have to offer and, whenever possible, it is wise to hire a caterer to handle the reception. He has the experience and the buying power to provide for the couple's needs at the least possible expense. Although in special circumstances it is possible for a caterer to plan and prepare a reception in less time, he should usually be engaged at least sixty days in advance. The caterer's services are often scheduled and arranged for at the same time the reception facilities are reserved. Before meeting with the caterer they select, the couple should know the number of invitations they plan to send and have an estimate of the number of guests who will probably attend and the number of out-of-town guests who will probably not attend. A deposit is usually required as the caterer's services are scheduled.

Ordering Invitations, Announcements, Napkins and Thank-you Cards

Since these four items can usually be ordered from the same place, it is wise to order them at the same time. It is better to order a slightly larger quantity of these items rather than

■ *Never let a fool kiss you—or a kiss fool you.*

to run short and have to order a second printing. Obviously, the guest list should be completed and updated before ordering printed items so an accurate count can be made. If a picture is to be used on the invitations, the invitation style should be selected before having the picture taken so the photographer can take the type and shape of picture needed for the invitations.

Ordering Flowers

The florist is very well-equipped to take care of all the floral needs for the reception. Floral arrangements, bouquets, boutonnieres, and corsages can be ordered to match the colors selected for the reception. It is important to meet early

with the florist so that he will be able to meet your needs in the best way possible. He has many options from which the couple may choose. For instance, they might consider using some of the lovely silk flowers available. Flowers may be ordered through the caterer as part of his "package" arrangement.

Purchasing Insurance

If the bride and groom already have their own life and accident insurance policies, the engagement period is a good time to check these policies and begin the procedure to have

---

■ *A woman worries about the future until she has a husband, but a man never worries about the future until he has a wife.* (Liselotte Pulver)

them changed to the new beneficiaries. They may wish to change ownership of life insurance policies too, so the wife will own the insurance on her husband, and he will own the policy on her. (This becomes important in later years for estate-planning purposes.) It is wise for new couples to have good life, health and accident insurance to cover the cost of unexpected problems which they might not otherwise be able to afford. If the couple is planning to start their family soon, it is important to purchase health insurance three to four months prior to their wedding because many policies have a waiting period before maternity coverage becomes effective. If considerable travel is involved for the reception, open house, and honeymoon, the couple should be sure they have adequate life and accident coverage.

Ordering the Wedding Cake

There are many varieties of lovely wedding cakes available. The cake may be ordered from a caterer, the local bakery, or a neighbor or friend who specializes in decorating wedding cakes. If fresh flowers are desired for the cake, the florist should be advised. Fresh flowers, when used, are usually added to the cake at the last minute, so the cake decorator and the florist should understand their responsibility to complete the cake and prepare it for display.

**Engaging and Meeting with Musicians
    for Selection of Music**

Music can be a lovely addition to a reception. If the ceremony is to be a civil one, the couple will probably also want music at their wedding. They may choose a soloist, pianist,

■*Love does not consist in gazing at each other, but in looking
    together in the same direction.*   (Saint Exupery)

organist, or other instrumentalist to perform at their reception. It is important to meet with the musician well in advance of the reception so that together they can select appropriate and favorite music and the performer will have ample time to prepare. A fee should be offered to the performing musicians. If this is refused, it is proper to give a gift of appreciation to the performers.

Finding A New Home

This is one of the most exciting tasks the couple must complete—arranging for their first home. It is wise to have this matter taken care of well in advance of the wedding. They should find a house or apartment that they can afford and

make the necessary arrangements to move in just before or after they return from their honeymoon.

Making Arrangements for School

If either or both of the couple are planning to attend school after the marriage, there are arrangements to be made before the wedding. The bride's records need to be changed to her new name. It they are attending college at the time of their wedding and plan to take some time off from school for a

■*There is only one thing for a man to do who is married to a woman who enjoys spending money, and that is to enjoy earning it.*

honeymoon, their absence should be talked over with their teachers and professors so they won't be penalized academically.

Making Job Arrangements

If either or both of the couple are presently employed and plan to keep their job after the wedding, they will need to arrange for time off with their employer for their wedding and honeymoon. They should also inform their employer well ahead of time if they plan to quit their job at the time of their marriage. If they need a new job after their wedding, it is wise to find the job and make arrangements to start as soon as they return from the honeymoon.

Having the Bridal Portrait Taken

This picture is usually taken by the same photographer chosen to take the wedding-day pictures. Having this portrait

■ *Beware of little expenses; a small leak will sink a great ship.*
(Franklin)

taken at least six weeks prior to the wedding allows time to choose proofs and get a glossy print processed for the newspaper deadline. The bride should plan for her hairstyle and make-up to be as natural and normal as possible. This isn't the time to try out a new extreme style.

Addressing Invitations

Invitations should be addressed about six weeks before the wedding, although they shouldn't be mailed that early. All invitations should be hand-addressed. Friends and relatives may be asked to help. The return address of the bride's parents may be embossed or stamped on the back of the envelope.

Purchasing Gifts

The bride and groom often present each other with a wedding gift as a remembrance and token of their love. This gift is normally a small piece of jewelry. Also, the bride and groom give gifts to all of their attendants. These gifts are customarily perfume, cologne, jewelry, picture frames, pen and pencil sets, etc., and are given usually at the wedding site. All of the bride's gifts to her attendants should be alike, and all of the groom's gifts to his attendants should be the same. If jewelry is given, it is often planned to be part of the wedding line costuming.

Making Arrangements for Out-of-Town Guests

It is the responsibility of the families of the bride and groom to arrange places for their out-of-town guests to stay. If possible, arrangements should be made for guests to stay at the home of the bride's or groom's family, or at the homes of friends and relatives. Otherwise, hotel or motel arrangements can be made. If this is the case, the bride and her family are responsible for paying the hotel bill for her bridesmaids and the groom is responsible for paying the hotel bill for his attendants.

■*Henry Ford, when asked on his fiftieth wedding anniversary to give his formula for a successful married life, replied that it was the same formula he had used to make his automobile so successful: "Stick to one model."*

Getting Serological (Blood) Tests

Most states require a blood test or a physician's medical certificate before the couple can be married. This should be taken care of within the month prior to the wedding so that the marriage license can be obtained with the valid results of the blood test.

Obtaining the Marriage License

The marriage license must be obtained in the state in which the marriage will take place. A blood test is usually required and the license can be obtained for a small fee from the county clerk's office. Whenever possible, the couple should go together to obtain their license.

Mailing Invitations

Invitations should all be mailed at the same time about one month to two weeks before the wedding. It's wise to double check the stack for complete and accurate addresses and stamps before mailing. In some areas, it is becoming acceptable for the bride and groom or the bride's family to hand deliver the invitations to neighborhood areas.

■ *You don't have to know how to sing; it's feeling as though you want to that makes the day successful.* (Monta Crane)

Writing Thank-you Notes as Early Gifts Arrive

Thank-you notes should be written and sent for gifts that arrive before the wedding, as soon as the gifts are received. By doing this, gifts will not be forgotten and those sending gifts will know that they are appreciated. Be sure that thank-you notes contain some aspect of "personal touch" that reflects the maturity and sincerity of the couple.

Being Available for Bridal Showers and Parties

From one month to two weeks before her wedding, the bride should make herself available for showers and parties held in her honor. These showers should not be given by members of the bride's or groom's immediate family, nor should they be too numerous. Brides don't have time to attend more than two showers. The mothers and sisters of the bride and groom aren't expected to bring gifts, although they sometimes do. The bride should be asked to make the guest list for the shower. Two hours is an appropriate length for a bridal shower. The bride should write thank-you notes for shower gifts and to shower hostesses immediately following the shower if time permits.

Arranging Transportation for the Bridal Party

It is important for the bride to make sure that all members of the bridal party have transportation to and from the wedding and the reception. The groom shall make similar arrangements if an open house is to be held.

Double Checking All Previous Arrangements

It is advisable to double check all previous arrangements three to four weeks before the wedding. This helps to keep last-minute problems from occurring.

■ *The honeymoon is over when he phones that he'll be late for supper and she's already left a note that it's in the refrigerator.*

Making Arrangements for the Honeymoon

Every newly-married couple should go on some kind of a honeymoon. Leaving out this important trip will bring regret in the years to follow as it never will be possible to recreate the same newness of experiences. The trip needn't be extravagant or expensive, but it does need to provide a chance for the two to be alone together. The groom is responsible for making the honeymoon arrangements. Although it is customary for these plans to remain quite private, some family members should have a complete itinerary for emergency purposes. If commercial travel is planned, a travel agent can be helpful in making plans. Arrangements should be taken care of about a month in advance of the wedding.

Ordering and Fitting Tuxedos

If tuxedos have been selected as the apparel for the male members of the wedding party, it is the responsibility of the groom to order the tuxedos and arrange for their fitting. This should be done about a month in advance of the wedding to prevent any problems of lack of availability for the type of tuxedos desired.

Registering with a Bridal Registry

Although not necessary, it is wise for the bride to register with a bridal registry at a local store convenient to most of her guests. Often a small gift is offered to the couple by the store when they register. At the bridal registry, the bride and groom may pick their china, stoneware, crystal, silverware, etc., and then guests may choose appropriate gifts from the selections the bride and groom have made. Time needs to be planned into the after-wedding schedule for the bride and groom to finalize any necessary exchanges and adjustments with the store. The bride's and groom's names will appear in the newspaper with the bridal registry about two weeks before the wedding.

■ *Loans and debts make worries and frets.* (W. G. Benham)

Planning a Budget

Starting out with a good financial plan is a must for all new couples. Since money is often in short supply for couples as they get married and begin their life together, it is important that they put their money to its best use. This can only be done by planning their budget together. If possible, before their wedding, the couple should assess their financial standing and come up with a practical budget that will work well for them and keep them out of debt. If this can't be done before the wedding, it should be done shortly thereafter.

Inviting Guests to the Temple

Two weeks prior to their temple ceremony, the couple should send handwritten invitations to those close friends and relatives they have selected to attend their wedding. These guests must have a current temple recommend and should be informed of the proper arrival time and apparel as found in the information received from the temple. It is the bride's and groom's prerogative to ask their guests to dress in white if they wish. Most of the sealing rooms in the temple are small and intimate. If more than twenty people will be in attendance at the ceremony, a larger room should be scheduled. The temple ceremony will take about 30 minutes if the couple is only being married that day. The temple will want the bride and groom there with their escorts earlier than the scheduled time. Guests should be advised to be on time to the temple. Wedding guests may be invited to participate in a picture-taking session afterwards.

Attendants' Gowns Completed

All of the attendants' gowns should be completed by two weeks before the wedding to prevent any last-minute problems.

Receiving Pre-Marital Counseling

It is wise for every young couple to arrange for pre-marital counseling as the time for their wedding approaches. They can

■*Minds are like parachutes—they function best when opened.*

arrange to talk to their bishop, parent, or a professional counselor.

Obtaining a Temple Recommend

An appointment should be scheduled for the bride and groom to meet with their respective Bishops. The Bishops will want to hold these interviews no more than one to two weeks before the scheduled wedding date. Even if they already hold a current temple recommend, the bride and groom both must have a special recommend for marriage.

Receiving Temple Endowments

Although a bride and groom can receive their temple endowments and be sealed in marriage on the same day, many individuals who live near a temple choose to receive their own temple endowments several days before their wedding. This is usually done within the week before the marriage date. This time should be a spiritual highlight and it is appropriate to celebrate the occasion with friends and family afterwards. The bride or groom will want to ask a person who previously has been through the temple to be his or her escort. It is wise to counsel with one's Bishop as to the advisability of receiving one's endowments early. If you are to receive your endowments on the day of your wedding, you should plan extra time for going through one of the two or three living endowment sessions held each day. The living endowment ceremony will take from three to four hours, and the bride and groom will be asked to be at the temple about an hour before the beginning of the session. Don't schedule your day so tightly that you don't have extra time to allow for delays in temple scheduling if they occur.

Sending the Wedding Announcement to the Newspaper

Although the wedding announcement is not seen in the newspaper until after the wedding takes place, the parents of

---

■ *A wedding is an event, but marriage is an achievement.*
                    In Tune with the Father (Suomi College)

the bride should deliver the article to the society editor of the local newspaper one week prior to the wedding. They should check with the newspaper well in advance as to the format they wish followed. Arrangements should also be made to pick up the pictures submitted with the articles after the announcement is printed.

Purchasing and Preparing Food

If the couple or the bride's family has hired a caterer, he will take care of the purchasing and preparation of food according to their specifications. Many caterers plan for 10% more than the number of guests contracted for to be able to guarantee feeding all of the guests.

Decorating The Reception Facility

Plan decorations for the entrance, the reception line area, the gift area, the food-service area, the performance area, and parking and walkway areas. Count costs carefully—it may be cheaper to have the reception catered, thus having the decoration items furnished, than to rent and/or build them yourself.

Should the Reception be a Do-it-Yourself Affair?

Before deciding to host their own wedding reception, the bride and groom and the bride's parents should check with the caterers in their area. They may very well find that a caterer can present the reception for less money than they could do it themselves. Certainly hiring a caterer will save much time and worry as this important and busy time approaches. A caterer can also present the reception in a professional manner, avoiding the errors that may occur if inexperienced people

---

■*Use it up, wear it out, make it do, or do without.*
(New England Maxim)

attempt to host such a major event. A caterer, with his whole-sale purchasing power, big planning experience, and his ability to use some leftover items for other events, can often save money, as contrasted to the individual who must purchase at full retail, often buys far too much because he doesn't know how to properly estimate the reception attendance, and must give away or throw away all unused food, etc.

However, the bride's family may elect to host the reception on a "do-it-yourself" basis. They would do well to enlist the help of many responsible friends and relatives, and clearly define their individual responsibilities many weeks in advance. The responsibility for the various major activities of the reception such as purchasing, decorating, kitchen and food preparation, food service, program and cleanup should be assigned to various individuals who are not members of the actual wedding party—the wedding events will occupy their attention at the same time as the reception preparation will require.

A reception is like a banquet, and requires the same staff, skills, and expertise. *Meals for Many—A Complete Guide to Banquets and Buffets for Groups of All Sizes,*[1] by Dr. Edward E. Sanders, is an excellent book that tells how to effectively host and stage such an event. It covers organizing for results, planning for success, budgeting and purchasing for economy, kitchen and food preparation, serving the food, and suggests menus and recipes for banquets and buffets. The principles it teaches can turn an amateur fiasco into a delightful event, and easily save hundreds of dollars of expense and dozens of hours of wasted time. The book is worth its weight in gold for anyone who is seriously considering a "do-it-yourself" reception.

Making Arrangements for Gifts

The decision of how to display the gifts should be made early in your plans for the reception. A responsible person should be asked to handle this, especially if you follow the local custom of having the gifts opened as they arrive. Great care should be taken to not mix up cards or allow damage to occur. A specific person should also be asked to move the

---

1. Available from *Horizon Publishers and Distributors,* P.O. Box 490, Bountiful, Utah, 84010. Write or call for current prices. Dr. Sanders is a university professor, a certified food executive, and the former manager of restaurants in one of the nation's major airports.

gifts to a place where they can be safely stored until the bride and groom return from their honeymoon.

If you follow the custom of having the gifts opened as they arrive, a responsible person should be asked to handle these items, taking great care not to mix up cards or allow damage to occur.

Packing Honeymoon Bags

Since it is customary to leave for the honeymoon directly from the reception, the bride and groom should have their bags packed before the wedding day and arrangements made to get the bags to the reception area.

Preparing the Car and Protecting It During the Reception

Although decorating the bride's and groom's car can be fun, if the decorating efforts are carried too far, damage can occur and the newlyweds' honeymoon departure can be delayed. If the bride and groom are concerned about possible trouble in this area, it may be wise for them to have their car in a friend's garage or a similar hiding place. In these circumstances, the fewer people who know where their car is, the better. They should remember to get any necessary repair work needed on their car early. This will avoid last minute emergencies or breakdowns on the honeymoon.

Registering the Marriage License

After the wedding, it is important to register the license at the county clerk's office. This provides the couple with legal evidence of marriage in case they should ever lose their marriage certificate. They should find out the procedure for registering the marriage when they buy their license. If it is a temple marriage, the temple personnel will see that the marriage license is properly registered.

■*The happiest marriages are those in which each partner thinks he or she got the best of it.*

Thanking Parents

As soon after the wedding as possible, the thoughtful bride and groom should express thanks to both of their parents. This can be done by a telephone call, telegram, flowers, or note of thanks.

Sending Thank-you Notes

It is the bride's responsibility to send sincere, well-composed handwritten thank-you notes to all those who have either given wedding gifts to the new couple or hosted parties in her honor. On cards written to close friends and relatives, the bride need only sign her first name. Other cards should be signed with her first name, maiden name, and surname. These cards should be sent as soon as possible, preferably within a month, and no later than three months after the wedding. All gifts given to the couple should be recorded in a gift book as they are received to facilitate ease in sending thank-you notes, and special care should be taken to see that all gifts and their givers are properly identified.

Stocking the Kitchen

After the wedding, it will be necessary to stock the apartment kitchen, not only with food, but with needed utensils

---

■*The best portion of a good man's life, his little, nameless, unremembered acts of kindness and of love.* (Wordsworth)

and appliances. Buying such items as toilet paper, laundry soap, and toothpaste before the wedding might help prevent some emergencies. It will take a substantial amount of money to stock a kitchen, so this will need to be budgeted into the couple's plans.

Selecting a Bank and Opening a Joint Account

It is wise for the new couple to select a good bank in which to put their money and to set up a joint account. This should be done immediately before or shortly after the wedding. Many banks offer special packages for newlyweds to encourage customers.

Suggested Planning Checklist

The following checklist will help the wedding day activities to run smoothly. It is suggested that a detailed schedule be prepared and reviewed with all who will be taking part in the full day's events.

4-6 months prior to the wedding:

1. Establish contact between the two families.

2. Have an initial interview with the Bishop.

3. Make the guest list.

4. Set the date for the wedding ceremony. (Make sure the temple will be open or the chapel available.)

5. Reserve the reception facilities.

6. Invite attendants to participate.

7. Announce the engagement in the newspaper (optional— 4 months ahead).

8. Schedule the wedding rehearsal, if necessary.

9. Order or begin construction of the wedding gown and attendants' gowns.

My interest is in the future, because I am going to spend the rest of my life there. (Charles Kettering)

10. Arrange for the out-of-town openhouse, if planned.

11. Prepare a wedding-reception budget.

2-4 months prior to the wedding:

1. Engage and meet with the caterer (or organize the needed committees for a "do-it-yourself reception). Plan decorations, menus, costs, etc.

2. Engage and schedule with photographer.

3. Order invitations, announcements, napkins, and thank-you cards.

4. Order flowers.

5. Investigate insurance.

6. Arrange for music.

7. Order cake.

8. Find a new home for the couple.

9. Make arrangements for school, if necessary.

10. Make job arrangements.

11. Make arrangements for the rehearsal or wedding dinner.

6 weeks prior to the wedding:

1. Have the wedding gown completed.

2. Have the bridal portrait taken (allow time to get glossy print processed for newspaper deadline).

3. Address invitations (do not mail yet).

4. Purchase gifts as needed (for bride, groom, attendants, and those who assist at wedding or reception or who give showers).

5. Make arrangements for out-of-town-guests.

■ *There's a difference between beauty and charm. A beautiful woman is one I notice. A charming woman is one who notices me.*   (John Erskine)

6. Schedule wedding ceremony time at the temple and make all related arrangements.

1 month prior to the wedding:

1. Get serological (blood) tests. (Must be dated within 30 days of marriage date.)

2. Have appointments with the doctor.

3. Obtain the marriage license.

4. Mail invitations. (About 2-3 weeks before the wedding date)

5. Write thank-you notes for gifts as they arrive.

6. Be available for bridal showers and parties.

7. Arrange for transportation for the bridal party, if needed.

8. Doublecheck all previous arrangements.

9. Groom makes arrangements for honeymoon.

10. Register with a bridal registry.

11. Groom orders and arranges for fitting of tuxedos.

12. Plan a budget for the first few months of the marriage.

2 weeks prior to the wedding:

1. Send invitations to those who are to be guests at the temple ceremony.

2. Have the attendants' gowns completed.

3. Receive pre-marital counseling.

4. Obtain temple recommends for the marriage.

1 week prior to the wedding:

1. Receive temple endowments, if desired.

2. Send the wedding announcement (with release date) to the newspaper.

■*A woman's mind is cleaner than a man's. She changes it more often.*

3. Pack the honeymoon bags.

4. Make arrangements for gifts to be stored.

5. Have the car serviced. Plan for protecting it during the reception.

6. Doublecheck with everyone to make sure no loose ends have been forgotten.

Day of the Wedding Checklist:

● Get to bed early the night before.

● Remember to take to the temple:
    Marriage license
    Temple recommends for everyone
    Wedding dress
    Temple clothes necessary

● Plan time for photographs at the temple.

● Have the wedding breakfast or luncheon.

● Plan for all wedding party to have time for a rest.

● Any gift delivery and decoration or food arrangements needed should be handled by people not involved too heavily with the wedding party.

After the wedding:

1. Register marriage license at county clerk's office.

2. Send telegram or note of thanks to both sets of parents.

3. Select bank and open joint account.

4. Stock the apartment kitchen.

5. Meet with bridal registry store to settle exchanges.

6. Send thank-you notes for all gifts received.

■*Sunday School Teacher: "Remember, brethren, when Lot's wife looked back, she turned into a pillar of salt."*
Brother Waters: "Last time my wife looked back, she turned into a lamp post."

7. Change insurance papers.

8. Relax!!

Division of Expenses

Over the years, traditions have been established which generally dictate the financial aspects of wedding etiquette. Though this division of expenses is varied in each case to meet the various needs of the participants, established custom is as follows:

Expenses of the bride and her parents:

1. Invitations.

2. Fees for buildings used.

3. Music.

4. Reception costs.

5. Photographer costs.

6. Bride's clothes and wedding gown.

7. Hotel bills for the bridesmaids, if necessary.

8. Flowers for the maid of honor, bridesmaids, and other attendants, and wedding line decorations.

9. A gift for the groom.

10. The groom's ring.

11. Gifts for those helping with the wedding or reception and for those who give showers for the bride.

12. Attendants' dresses, if desired (it is proper to ask brides maids to pay for their own dresses if the bride can't afford it or if the dresses will be useable on other occasions).

■*Life is easier to take than you think; all that is necessary is to accept the impossible, do without the indispensable, and bear the intolerable.*   (Kathleen Norris)

Expenses of the groom:

1. The bride's engagement and wedding rings.
2. Marriage license.
3. Bride's bouquet.
4. Corsages for both mothers and special relatives.
5. Boutonnieres for himself, the best man, ushers and both fathers.
6. Wedding clothes.
7. Gifts for the best man and ushers.
8. A gift for the bride.
9. Hotel bills for the best man and ushers, if necessary.
10. The honeymoon trip.
11. Tuxedos for attendants, if desired (it is proper to ask attendants to pay for their own tuxedos if the groom can't afford it).

Expenses of the groom's parents:

1. The wedding breakfast.
2. The openhouse, if bride is from out-of-town.

Approximate Price Ranges for Reception Catering

Every caterer has his own special "packages" and has established the prices he must charge, so the following can serve as only a rough estimate. In today's double-digit inflation these prices will probably increase about 15% per year. (These prices reflect the current costs in the Salt Lake City area in mid-1980 as this booklet goes to press.)

The following prices are averages for a catered reception at a rented reception center in which the caterer has taken

---

■*One way to get high blood pressure is to go mountain climbing over molehills.*

care of invitations, napkins, thank-you cards, guest books, the wedding cake, food, flowers, decorations, and photography.

200 guests or under	$ 300.00 to $ 500.00
300 guests.............	$ 500.00 to $ 700.00
400 guests.............	$ 900.00 to $1,100.00
600 guests.............	$1,200.00 to $1,500.00

At an average reception, 400 to 600 guests will attend.

Payment for a reception such as the above is usually made with a non-refundable deposit when the caterer is hired with the balance due either before the wedding or on the night of the reception. Payments are rarely allowed to remain uncollected after the reception night. One enterprising reception center host has a policy of padlocking the gift room until payment has been received, if it is not tendered on the reception night as agreed.

■*A crowd is not company, and faces are but a gallery of pictures, and talk about a tinkling cymbal, where there is no love.*   (Bacon)

Your Personal Schedule

The following checklist will help you to plan your personal schedule:

	Scheduled Completion Date	✔
Establish contact between the two families.	1-14-87	✓
Make preliminary wedding, reception, honeymoon plans.	_____	—
Bride—have an initial interview with her bishop.	12/28/86	✓
Groom—have an initial interview with his Bishop.	12/28/86	✓
Bride and her mother prepare their guest list.	_____	—
Groom and his mother send their guest list to the bride's mother.	_____	—
Organize the guest list card file or other system.	_____	—
Set the date and time for the wedding ceremony.	86-19-87	✓
Clear the date with the temple, or	_____	—
Arrange for the chapel or other location.	_____	—
Arrange for the person to perform the wedding ceremony.	_____	—
Decide whether the reception will be catered or "do-it-yourself."	_____	—
Schedule the reception and reserve the reception facilities.	1/4/87	—
Schedule the wedding rehearsal (if one is to be held).	N/A	—
Schedule, arrange facilities for the rehearsal dinner (if to be held).	N/A	—
Schedule, arrange facilities for the wedding breakfast or luncheon.	_____	—

■*Women have more imagination than men. They need it to tell us how wonderful we are.*   (Arnold Glasgow)

	Scheduled Completion Date	✔
Bride—choose and invite maid of honor, bridesmaids, flower girl.	_____	_
Groom—choose and invite best man, ushers.	_____	_
Announce the engagement in the newspaper.	*N/A*	_
Choose the style and/or pattern of the wedding dress.	_____	_
Choose the color scheme and dress style for the wedding party.	_____	_
Order or begin sewing of the wedding gown.	_____	_
Order or begin sewing of the attendants' gowns.	_____	_
Schedule and arrange for out-of-town openhouse facilities.	_____	_
Prepare a wedding reception budget.	_____	_
Engage and meet with the caterer, or organize reception (and openhouse) committees.	_____	_
Plan menus.	_____	_
Plan decorations, gift display.	_____	_
Plan printing.	_____	_
Plan flowers.	_____	_
Estimate reception (and openhouse) attendance.	_____	_
Groom—make honeymoon reservations (if needed).	_____	_
Schedule the photographer.	_____	_
Order invitations/announcements.	_____	_

■ *Faults are thick where love is thin.*

	Scheduled Completion Date	✔
Order thank-you cards.	_____	—
Order napkins.	_____	—
Order flowers.	_____	—
Arrange for insurance.	_____	—
Arrange for music for wedding, reception.	_____	—
Order the cake.	_____	—
Find a new home for the couple.	_____	—
Arrange for bride, groom to move out of their apartments.	_____	—
Make school arrangements.	_____	—
Make job arrangements for time off.	_____	—
Complete the wedding gown.	_____	—
Have the bridal portrait taken.	_____	—
Check portrait proofs, place picture order.	_____	—
Pick up invitations/announcements, other printed items.	_____	—
Address invitations/ announcements.	_____	—
Bride—purchase gifts as needed.	_____	—
Groom—purchase gifts as needed.	_____	—
Make housing, transportation arrangements for out-of-town guests.	_____	—
Make actual temple arrangements, finalize scheduling.	_____	—

■*Money is a terrible master but an excellent servant.*

	Scheduled Completion Date	✔
Bride—have blood test.	_____	—
Groom—have blood test.	_____	—
Bride—have physical examination, doctor counseling.	_____	—
Groom—have physical examination, doctor counseling.	_____	—
Obtain the marriage license.	_____	—
Mail, deliver invitations/ announcements.	_____	—
Invite dinner, breakfast, or luncheon guests.	_____	—
Set up a system for receiving and recording gifts.	_____	—
Write thank-you notes for gifts as they arrive.	_____	—
Bride—Be available for bridal showers and parties.	_____	—
Arrange for transportation for the bridal party.	_____	—
Doublecheck all previous arrangements.	_____	—
Groom—finalize and check honeymoon arrangements.	_____	—
Register with a bridal registry.	_____	—
Groom—order tuxedos and arrange for fittings.	_____	—
Plan budget for the first few months of marriage.	_____	—
Invite wedding ceremony guests.	_____	—
Complete attendants' gowns.	_____	—
Receive pre-marital counseling.	_____	—

■*Courtship is the moonlight of love. Marriage, the light bill.*

	Scheduled Completion Date	✓
Bride—obtain temple recommend for the wedding.	_____	__
Groom—obtain temple recommend for the wedding.	_____	__
Receive temple endowment, if desired.	_____	__
Write, send wedding announcement, photo to the newspaper.	_____	__
Pack, prepare to move out of apartment.	_____	__
Pack the honeymoon bags.	_____	__
Make arrangements for gifts to be stored.	_____	__
Have the car serviced.	_____	__
Arrange for the car to be protected during reception.	_____	__
Review this list. Double check all items.	_____	__
Enjoy the wedding!	_____	__

■ *Before marriage, a man will lie awake all night thinking about something you said. After marriage, he'll fall asleep before you finish saying it.*   (Helen Rowland)

There are a multitude of other specific details that must be handled as wedding is being planned. The following space is provided for these details to be listed.

Scheduled
Completion Date   ✔

_____ _____ __

_____ _____ __

_____ _____ __

_____ _____ __

_____ _____ __

_____ _____ __

_____ _____ __

_____ _____ __

_____ _____ __

_____ _____ __

_____ _____ __

_____ _____ __

_____ _____ __

_____ _____ __

_____ _____ __

■ *Two things are necessary to keep a wife happy. First, let her think she's having her way. Second, let her have her way.*

	Scheduled Completion Date	✔
_____	_____	__
_____	_____	__
_____	_____	__
_____	_____	__
_____	_____	__
_____	_____	__
_____	_____	__
_____	_____	__
_____	_____	__
_____	_____	__
_____	_____	__
_____	_____	__
_____	_____	__
_____	_____	__
_____	_____	__

■_An archeologist is the best husband any woman can have; the older she gets, the more interested he is in her._
(Agatha Christie)

	Scheduled Completion Date	✓
_____	_____	—
_____	_____	—
_____	_____	—
_____	_____	—
_____	_____	—
_____	_____	—
_____	_____	—
_____	_____	—
_____	_____	—
_____	_____	—
_____	_____	—
_____	_____	—
_____	_____	—
_____	_____	—
_____	_____	—
_____	_____	—

■*Show me a married couple who boast they've never had an argument and I'll show you a pair of lovebirds, complete with birdbrains.*

Plan Your Wedding Budget

	Month	Month	Month	Month
Income				
Total Income				

Expenses				
Contacts between families				
Inviting attendants to par-ticipate				
Newspaper announcements				
Wedding gown				
Attendants' gowns				
Photographer				

■ *Patience is that art of concealing your impatience.*

Caterer			
Printer			
Florist			
Insurance			
Musicians			
Invitations: postage			
Gifts: bride and groom			
Gifts: attendants			
Lodging out-of-town guests			
Medical exams			
Marriage license			
Thank-you notes, postage			
Reception: building			
Reception: decorations			
Reception: food			
Wedding cake			
Wedding breakfast			
Open house: building			
Open house: decorations			
Open house: food			

■*United we stand, divided we fall.*   (Aesop)

Travel expenses				
Food expenses while traveling				
Tuxedos				
Car Repair				
Honeymoon: travel				
Honeymoon: lodging				
Honeymoon: food				
Honeymoon: misc.				
Bride's clothing				
Groom's clothing				
Apartment: move-out expenses				
Apartment: move-in expenses				
Telephone				
Total Expenses				

■*A man-of-the-hour is the one whose wife told him to wait a minute.*

Notes

_____

_____

_____

_____

_____

_____

_____

_____

_____

_____

_____

_____

_____

_____

_____

_____

_____

■*Adversity borrows its sharpest sting from your impatience.*
(Bishop Horne)

Notes

_____

_____

_____

_____

_____

_____

_____

_____

_____

_____

_____

_____

_____

_____

_____

_____

_____

_____

■*Many a man is poor today because his credit rating was excellent yesterday.*